D1542280

To my wonderful, supportive, and loving mother, Mona Rappaport. To my beautiful sister, incredible photojournalist Linda Solomon. To my dear Rick Swift, for his love and support for all my "Fur Angels." And to my Sweet Pea, Buckaroo, CJ, Petey, Madison, Oreo, Sundance, Bella, Ranger, Wishbone, Lakota, Hannah, and Kay, who by being in my life make it so much better. And to everyone who has ever adopted and/or rescued a precious animal and given him or her a wonderful, loving home: bless you. —Jill Rappaport

In memory of my father, Pete Minneti, who loved animals and orchestrated this journey. —Lynea Lattanzio

For Linda, Garth, Katie, and Sofie. —Bob Carey

Collins is an imprint of HarperCollins Publishers.

500 Cats
Text copyright © 2009 by Jill Rappaport with Lynea Lattanzio
Photographs copyright © 2009 by Bob Carey
Manufactured in China.
All rights reserved. No part of this book may be used or reproduced in any manner whatsoever without written permission except in the case of brief quotations embodied in critical articles and reviews. For information address HarperCollins Children's Books, a division of HarperCollins Publishers, 10 East 53rd Street, New York, NY 10022.
www.harpercollinschildrens.com

Library of Congress Cataloging-in-Publication Data
Rappaport, Jill. 500 cats / by Jill Rappaport with Lynea Lattanzio ; photographs by Bob Carey.
— 1st ed.   p. cm. ISBN 978-0-06-179909-9 (trade bdg.) — ISBN 978-0-06-179910-5 (lib. bdg.)
1. Cats—Juvenile literature. 2. Animal sanctuaries—California—Parlier—Juvenile literature.
I. Lattanzio, Lynea. II. Carey, Bob, date ill. III.
Title. IV. Title: Five hundred cats. SF445.7.R356 2009
2009001266   636.8—dc22   CIP   AC   Design by Stephanie Bart-Horvath
09 10 11 12 13   SCP   10 9 8 7 6 5 4 3 2 1
❖
First Edition

500 CATS

BY **JILL RAPPAPORT**
WITH **LYNEA LATTANZIO**
PHOTOGRAPHS BY **BOB CAREY**

Collins
An Imprint of HarperCollins Publishers

Hi!
I'm Mittens,
a very lucky
kitten.

Once I was lost and alone.
Then someone kind found me.
While I wait for a family
to give me a new home,
I'm staying in a very special place

because . . .

500 cats!

I'm curious.
There's so much to see and explore
when you live with 500 cats.

I'm with Ellie.

I'm following Feather.

It's not only cats.
Dogs live here too.
Ellie and Feather are my pals.

Rumble. Grumble.
That's my stomach.
It must be lunchtime.
There are enough bowls
and food for 500 cats.

When it's playtime . . .

I can always find playmates
picking from . . .

500 cats.

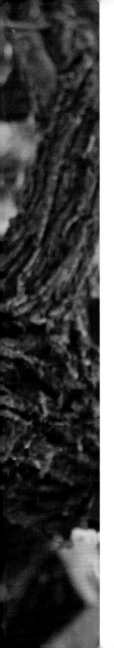

There is space to run
and tumble and even
climb high.

Look at me, up in a tree!

When it's nap time,
sleepy cats are
everywhere.

I find the *purrfect* spot
to dream *sweet* dreams!

I'm a very happy kitten.
And a lucky one too.
Until I'm adopted
by someone kind,
I'll be safe and loved,
living together with . . .

500 cats.

The Cat House on the Kings

When Jill Rappaport—longtime Emmy-nominated animal welfare and entertainment correspondent for NBC's *Today* show—saw the short documentary film on YouTube about the Cat House on the Kings, she was fascinated by the cat paradise and amazed that so many cats and dogs could live together peacefully. She was inspired to write a book imagining what it might be like for a kitten to arrive there and meet hundreds of cats inside, outside, in the grass, in the trees, asleep. Everywhere!

A well-known animal lover, Jill is the author of the *New York Times* bestseller *People We Know, Horses They Love* and *Mazel Tov: Celebrities' Bar and Bat Mitzvah Memories*. Her first book for children, *Jack & Jill: The Miracle Dog with a Happy Tail to Tell*, is the touching story of how she rescued an abandoned German shepherd puppy and cared for him through sickness and recovery. Jack's incredible life and strong will to live changed Jill's life forever. A portion of the proceeds from her new clothing line for Pendleton will benefit the Jack & Jill Rappaport National Awareness Campaign for animals with cancer, in association with the American College of Veterinary Internal Medicine and Tails of Hope Foundation, Inc. Jill loves spending time with her four dogs and seven horses on her ranch in Water Mill, New York.

Lynea Lattanzio runs the largest no-cage sanctuary for cats and dogs in California. For more than seventeen years, thousands of cats and dogs have roamed the twelve acres of the Cat House on the Kings, waiting to be found by owners who will give them a permanent home. Lynea says, "If they don't have a home, at least they have a life. . . . It's not a life if they're in a cage."

Bob Carey is a New York–based photographer who specializes in conceptual and environmental portraiture. He is the photographer of the picture book *A Home for Dixie*. In addition to gallery shows, he has contributed to publications such as *O*, *Essence*, *Diane*, and *Men's Health*. When he found out about the sanctuary, he couldn't wait to meet the cats either! He traveled across the country to get up close and personal with 500 cats.

Nate Woodruff

Bob

Lynea

Pat Miranda

Jill & Jack

Linda Solomon